Bird Eating Spiders

A Complete Bird Eating Spider Pet Owner's Guide

Bird Eating Tarantula breeding, where to buy, types, care, temperament, cost, health, handling, diet, and much more included!

By: Lolly Brown

Foreword

Bird eating spiders are the kind of spiders that creeps you out in your dreams or perhaps your nightmares. Many people are afraid of these spider species including its other relatives in the tarantula family; rightfully so because tarantulas are the biggest species in the arachnid clan. They are big "killing" animals that can perfectly adapt to their environments – either in the wild or in captivity.

Bird eating spiders are one of the largest and scariest of all the spider species under the tarantula family – probably because of their size, and their abilities. They have fangs that measures about an inch in length, and when their legs are fully spread, it can measure to about 1 foot! This creature is usually distributed in the rainforests in of South America and the northern region of Australia.

They are big and they can also bite, but they're not dangerous to humans. Their bite is no worse than when a bee stings you. That being said, this creature is not meant to be kept as pets for the faint at heart but if you want to turn fear into fascination, then you'll need this book to get off the topic of their fangs and get on with the facts!

Table of Contents

Introduction

The bird eating spider is a revertible huge species. Its body has a maximum length of 55 millimeters and its leg span reaches about 160 millimeters. The bird eating spider is considered as tropical spider specie that's mostly distributed and widespread in the northern region of Australia. These species dwells on the ground and loves to burrow with a depth that reaches about 1 meter deep mainly on the left side facing east. They are known for preying on medium to relatively large animals such as small reptiles, frogs, huge insects, centipedes, big cockroaches, large worms, and snails that are found near their lair's entrance. These bird eating spiders love to get tangled around their silk - colored sheet of web which is usually spread on their burrow's entrance.

Introduction

Their main physical difference from other spider species is their par exile fangs as opposed to the common fangs found in other spiders. Their fangs are quite similar to a snake which measures around 8 1/2 millimeters in length - a truly formidable weapon for this 8 legged creature. They're not dangerous to humans but if you're bitten by one, you might end up pretty ill. According to zoologist, if a bird eating spider bit a human, he/she can vomit for about 6 hours. So better be careful whenever you're handling them. For a small animal like a bird or other small reptiles, it will only take about 30 minutes for them to die after being bitten by this giant bird eating spider. The bird eating spider species are under the family of tarantulas which means that they are capable of climbing glass or walls.

Find out more about the Giant Bird Eating Spider in this book and learn what it would take for you to acquire one, keep one in your home, feed it, and how you can enjoy caring for it in captivity. This book will introduce you to one of the largest spider species of the tarantula family! Learn more about this goliath sized arachnid to help you make a decision if this is the right hairy species for you and your family. Get ready to put your fangs on!

Chapter One: Biological Information of Bird Eating Spiders

Most creatures in the wild use camouflage as a defense against potential threats and predators, but if it's not an option, then the only thing left is to hold your ground – just like the giant bird eating spider. They appear wild and scary but they can be kept as pets. If you're a spider enthusiast or someone who has the guts to take care of one of these big and hairy eight – legged creatures then this might be the spider species for you. This chapter will cover the physical and behavioral characteristics of the giant bird eating spider.

Understanding Bird Eating Spiders

The bird eating spider's legs measures about 1 foot long, enough to cover a person's head. Its name is also very far from the truth; it usually prows on small and large insects in the wild and also the occasional medium – sized animals like rodents and frogs. Its fangs are about 1 inch long that are packed with neurotoxins that's injected into its dying prey. The venom secreted by this spider is fatal to most animals in the jungle.

After capturing its prey, the bird eating spider will now take its prey into its lair or burrow. Their lair is like a silk welcome mat, and sort of acts like a trip wire, once a possible prey gets within range, the bird eating spider will know even if it's tucked away in its burrow – thanks to its spider webs. The spider will then proceed on sucking all of the liquids in its prey's body before sucking its meal dry. However, just like any other animals in the jungle, this fearsome predator has of course its own set of threats. There are mammals like tigers and reptiles like snakes that can easily eat the bird eating spider and other similar tarantula creatures.

The problem with most spiders is that it has very poor eyesight despite of their eight eyes, which is one major disadvantage especially if these creatures are out there in the wild. The bird eating spider only relies to its vibration –

sensitive hairs to warn it against potential threats. If ever they come face to face with a predator and has no other way to get out, they'll use their other secret weapon – a long range one. Bird eating spiders have many spiky and very tiny hairs on its body which are tipped with stinging barbs. What they do is they rub their legs so that these tiny hair flicks up into the air like clouds of mini missiles, these tiny missiles can burn the eyes, nose or mouth of their potential predators.

The bird eating spiders are usually nocturnal animals, and even if they're like to ambush their prey, they also know the safest way of hunting – which is to sit there, and wait for the right time. "Let the enemy come to you" is perhaps their feeding technique and one of their greatest strengths.

Bird Eating Spider Facts and Physical Features

- Other names include: Goliath bird eater, Giant tarantula, and Giant bird eater. Obviously, it got its nicknames due to its enormous size. They are the biggest and heaviest spider species in the world with an average weight of 170 grams (6 oz).

- Bird – eating spiders only prey on small birds occasionally, they were called "bird – eating" because a zoologist named Maria Merian, who discovered this animal species, was seen eating a humming bird at the time around the 18th century. The name sort of got stuck to it.

- Like most tarantulas, the giant bird eating spiders have many sensitive hairs on all of its 8 legs. They are arachnid creatures that don't have any inner skeleton structure or a backbone. They have exoskeleton which can be described as a hard outer covering or an outer skeletal framework.

- The bird eating spider is a ground dwelling spiders which are also adept climbers. Their legs are equip with suction - like cups able to produce a substance which allows them to climb any sort of surface with ease, with no need for web weaving.

- The giant bird eating spider will tend to shed its outer skeletal structure every now and then (a process called molting), so that it can grow and create a new set of exoskeleton.

- Molting allows spiders to grow and also repair its broken legs. It's a regeneration ability. Once the new limb is formed, it usually appears small and underdeveloped at first but as time goes by, it will slowly increase in size and also gain mass after each molting season until it reaches its normal size.

- Female giant bird eating spiders are usually bigger in terms of size than males, and they also tend to have a longer life span.

- Usually, male bird eating spiders die quite some time after reaching their sexual maturity. Most male bird eating spider species only lasts for about 3 to 6 years. Females tent to lasts for a very long time even in the wild; they can live up to around 25 years or longer.

- Females undergo through the process of molting throughout their lifetime compared to male spiders.

Male species tend to stop molting once they've reach their maturity.

- You can identify a male bird eating spider by looking at their physical characteristics. Males have matting hooks that can be found in their forelegs. Females don't have that kind of hooks.

- Male bird eating spiders tends to have an inability to molt after it comes into sexual maturity. This means that if they cannot molt, they won't be able to regenerate and renew its body parts like its palps and legs.

- Its fangs measures about 2 ½ inches which is equal to the length of a cheetah's claws, this is why penetrating a human skin can be very easy.

- The venom from their fangs can be fatal to most animals, and can cause nausea, vomiting, and severe pain to humans.

Bird Eating Spider Behavioral Features

- Giant bird eating spiders usually create a hissing sound whenever it feels threatened, and it is done by rubbing its legs very rapidly which then produces the miniature missile like spiky hairs that can protect him from predators.

- When it comes to defense mechanisms, the first line of defense for the bird eating spider is to retreat or withdraw from a potential predator or attacker. It will also produce a hissing sound by rubbing rows of tiny spines or hair – like spins around their hind legs or near the bulky area of their body. This is where the hissing sound comes from not in its mouth.

- If fleeing or the hissing sound it creates doesn't ward off the enemy, the bird eating spider will launch this tiny missile - like hairs/ spines onto its attacker. The tarantula kicks these miniature hairs by rubbing its back legs repeatedly against its abdomen in the direction of the predator.

- Baby spiders have been seen eating insects provided by their mother. This is evidence that the spiders are somewhat intelligent because they know what needs to be done.

- When it comes to feeding; in the wild bird eating spiders are known to be general eaters with relatively healthy appetites. In captivity, a bird eating spider may be fed pinkies or other insects like grasshoppers, crickets, earthworms, and even cockroaches to name a few.

- Like most tarantulas, bird eating spiders molt periodically. They shed and get rid of their exoskeletons so they may grow a new one. As mentioned earlier this is also their way to regenerate and repair broken legs, replace stomach linings as well as the female genitalia. They are also able to regrow their pedipalps.

- Molting also signals that the spider is preparing itself for breeding. The period of molting is extremely stressful to a tarantula species like the bird eating spider, which is why during this period, they should not be disturbed nor should they be offered food like a live prey as they may not be in their best condition to chomp down another animal.

Taxonomy, Origin and Distribution

These animals have a scientific name of *Theraphosa Blondi*. It belongs to Kingdom Animalia, Phylum Arthropoda, Class Arachnida, Order Araneae, Family Theraphosidae, Genus Theraphosa, Species Blondi.

Giant bird eating spiders are usually distributed in rainforests and wild jungles in southern America, northern Australia, northern Brazil, Venezuela, Guyana, and French Guiana. They inhabit burrows left by rodents/ rats, and build their sets of webs and trip – like wires in it. They are ambush predators that spews venom kill their prey which can also dissolve all the internal organs of the prey so that it can easily be digested by the spider in liquid form.

In the wild, they feed on earthworms, small insects, rodents, lizards, earthworms, small birds as well as other kinds of amphibians and reptiles.

Chapter Two: Bird Eating Spiders as Pets

In many countries around the world, you can find lots of bird eating spiders for sale as house pets. This creature is becoming quite popular especially among spider hobbyists who already have prior experience of taking care of tarantulas. As amazing and fascinating as they are, bird eating spiders are not a good choice as pets especially for newbie owners or for young kids. This is because they are huge and they are very long and heavy with dangerous fangs and stinging venom. They are quite wild and having them as pets especially if you're a first time keeper might not be a good idea.

Bird eating spiders are quite aggressive and can spell trouble if you don't have an expert who'll guide you. Nevertheless, if you're as wild as these huge creatures are, and you're interested in keeping them then this chapter will provide you with everything you need.

Conservation and Licensing

The IUCN or the International Union for Conservation of Nature hasn't evaluated yet the current population of giant bird eating tarantulas. Although in the past, the population of these animals is relatively stable but from time to time it's experiencing a constant threat to its survival, this is because many bird eating spiders are being captured for illegal pet trade. Capturing these aggressive bird eating spiders in the wild is very dangerous and difficult which is why pet traders usually risk themselves for getting stung by its venom but the reason that they do that is because whenever they catch one of these big spiders they can sell it for bigger profits. Adult female bird eating spiders can lay thousands of eggs in their lifetime that's why they are being captured more than males.

Another threat to conservation of these species is deforestation and loss of habitat. In some countries, locals also hunt these animals because it has been part of their cuisine since ancient times. Even though the population right now is stable, zoologists are still saying that their population might get threatened and endangered in the future.

When it comes to licensing or getting permits, it is best that you acquire one since licensing systems aid in the protection of wildlife from aggressive exploitation as well as the negative impacts to exotic species such as the bird eating spiders in a particular region.

Acquiring licenses ensure that the populations of wild plants and animals remain viable. These licensing systems are also in place and should be heeded to help maintain in keeping, taking, using and transport of wildlife for recreational, commercial or other purposes under monitor. This is use to protect illegal collection of some species from the wild, as mentioned earlier, bird eating tarantulas have been harvested from the wild by illegal traders, and are said to be threatened by the wrath of mother nature. It is best to only acquire a bird eating tarantulas that have been bred in captivity to dissuade unscrupulous hunters from snatching them out of their lairs.

If you plan on acquiring one or more of these bird eating spiders, then you should check with your local animal or pet organization to determine if owning one would need licensure in your state or place of residence. Even if there are no state laws regarding pet spiders, it is highly advised that you check in your town or village if there are any rules because these might provide further regulations regarding pet spiders even when state law otherwise allows it.

How Many Bird Eating Spiders Should You Keep?

If you already have an experience in keeping tarantulas or other spider species, then it'll be easy for you to keep more than one of these creatures. According to arachnid enthusiasts, if you wanted to keep more than one or even just one, then you should be physically and financially prepared to care for each one of these spiders.

You must have sufficient space to house each one of the spiders, and you should be financially prepared and able to support and provide for all their needs. Ideally, you should house your pets in separate encasements to avoid attacks, fights and the potential to prey on one another. Most tarantulas like the bird eating spiders are predators by nature, and taming them from eating their own kind can be next to impossible because it is in their nature to prey on different species even their own kind. You as a keeper should also ensure that you monitor all of them and provide them with enough attention in terms of food and husbandry.

If you really are aiming to keep more than one bird eating spider or any kind of spider for that matter, make sure you have assigned specific enclosures for each of them. Regardless of what information you may gather about each species and how they treat each other, one can never be sure when it comes to individual spiders especially the ones kept in captivity, and in close proximity to each other.

Never attempt a communal setup unless you have done extensive research and have several years of experience in keeping and caring for these kinds of pet. Setting up a multiple specie enclosure is the way to go but it can be quite difficult to set up even with thoughtful planning. Each inhabitant will require specific climate control that is designed specifically for their needs unless of course you're keeping the same kind.

The behavior and traits of the animals will also have to be taken into consideration to gauge compatibility. Mesh wires may have to be used to separate the animals from each other. A multi species terrarium housing two or more arachnid or bird eating spiders will have to be quite large to accommodate each of the creatures which are separated by individual enclosures. You should be able to monitor the terrarium very closely to make sure the temperature and overall conditions is right for each of the inhabitants' needs.

Do Bird Eating Spiders Get Along with Other Pets?

If you think tarantulas will be friends with your other household pets like reptiles or mammals, then you should be prepared for some kind of bloodshed. Keep in mind that tarantulas are cannibals, and if you decide to house your pet with other species there will surely fight to the death. Worst case scenario would be the hobbyist coming in for a visit only to find out that your spider already sucked the life out of the other occupants.

It's also best to quarantine your pet especially if you didn't acquire it from a reputable breeder as it can come directly from the wild. Testing and treating each animal for the presence of parasite and/or harmful pathogens will be very costly. It will also take much more work if each animal were housed separately in their own enclosures.

Costs of Keeping a Bird Eating Spider

As mentioned earlier, part of being a responsible keeper is being able to provide for the spider's needs. You should be financially prepared if you want to keep these kinds of creatures especially if you're going to acquire a female bird eating spider since they can live for a very long time. This section will give you an overview of the initial costs in keeping bird eating spiders.

Purchase Price

The cost of acquiring a bird eating spider from a reputable breeder can range in price depending on its availability. You can expect to pay from as little as $10 or less for slings, and as much as $90 for juvenile or full grown bird eating tarantulas.

Enclosure

Since bird eating spiders are huge species, you may need to really invest in a good quality and large terrarium. Keep in mind that this is where your pet will build its house of webs, and this is the place where he/she will stay for a very long time. The enclosure should have a secure lid on top and preferably made out of glass so that you can monitor it well and also something that will blend in well among your furniture. Depending on the type and size of the terrarium it can cost around$5 (for slings), and between $50 and $100 for adult size or full size enclosures.

Other Cage Decorations

You'll also need to provide cage decors inside the enclosure to ensure that it resembles their habitat in the wild. You need to buy substrate, sphagnum moss, coconut bedding, heat pads, and plastic ornaments where they'll build their webs.

Pros and Cons of Keeping Bird Eating Spiders

Just like any other pets, keeping bird eating spiders have their own sets of pros and cons. Generally speaking, you need to be prepared and committed when it comes to keeping these kinds of pets, you should also have enough money to buy everything they need, and also have enough time to monitor them and care for them. You would also need to invest a lot of your time (initially) to ensure that your bird eating spider is comfortable, well – provided, secured, and happy in its new environment. Here are the pros and cons of keeping one:

Pros

- Bird eating spiders are the largest tarantula species
- If you're someone who's extremely fascinated with these 8 legged creatures and how they live, then this is the right one for you
- If you like to see them burrowing underground or climbing up on the glass.

- They like to show off their fangs and has an ability to make hissing sounds
- It can be a great pest control agent since they love eating roaches, and other smaller insects.
- They are great pets to keep especially for an experienced hobbyist.

Cons

- Bird eating spiders are not ideal for first time spider keepers
- They can be difficult to handle
- They are very aggressive, they can bite, and they are also venomous
- Not suitable for very young children
- If bitten, it can make you pretty sick with symptoms of nausea and vomiting. If you get stung, it can cause skin irritating and itchiness
- They are not friendly with other creatures even of their own kind. Their bite can also be fatal to your other household pets.

Chapter Three: How to Acquire a Bird Eating Spider

There are a lot of experienced keepers who can attest to the inhumane ways of how bird eating spiders and other tarantula species are acquired in the wild. Purchasing an arachnid species from illegal traders is highly discouraged because it contributes to the depletion of the species population in the wild. Purchasing young spiders that are bred in captivity is better because aside from its environmental advantages, it also assures you that the spider was kept in conditions where it wouldn't have been exposed to pathogens and parasites as those caught in the wild.

If you purchase a spider from an illegal trader, chances are that the spider will be much more aggressive since it is wired to react as if it's in the wild. You'll have a hard time keeping them and also handling or feeding them as they are not raised in captivity. With the advent of the internet and various online communities, prospective keepers now have several options in looking for a place to buy their future pet. You'll learn where you can acquire your pet in this chapter.

Reminders When Choosing Where to Buy

There are many countless hobbyists and breeders with years of experience and success in breeding bird eating tarantula species which is why it's highly recommended that you buy from these kinds of reputable breeders to ensure that you'll get a healthy breed, help conserve and protect its population, and also get lessons from the experienced keepers as you go through this journey with your new found pet. Here are some reminders to keep in mind when purchasing a bird eating spider:

- **Search online and read the reviews.** Reading testimonials of people who have already bought tarantulas from specific breeders is a must so that you have an idea of the type of breeder/s you'll be dealing with. This is how you can shortcut the whole searching process because you'll get past the advertisements and all the positive things that these breeders post about themselves or their breeds online. Previous customers will help you gauge if this is a reputable breeder and someone who'll help you even after the spider breed is sold.

- **Check various forums or join groups online.** Thanks to the internet, you can now get recommendations from people about where to buy and not to buy. Never order a spider online without asking where it came from especially if the cost seems unusually high because this could mean that the spiders are hunted in the wild, sold cheap to the distributor, and you getting charged more than the standard price. Ask for recommendations and from there do your own comparison.

- **See it for yourself!** Once you have prospective breeder, it's best to come to their place or breeding facility if any so that you'll have an idea of how these spiders were raised. However, if the breeder is located far from where you are, then you can just do phone interviews to see if they are really legit. Make sure to also visit their website, and ask for pictures of the breed, and if possible a video to get a sort of sneak peak on how they raised these creatures. This is the only way to determine if they are reputable since you cannot travel long distances to visit their facilities.

- **Ask away!** Don't hesitate to ask questions especially the important ones. If they are a reputable and passionate breeder, they'll understand your inquisitive nature. They must also be polite enough to answer all of your questions, and perhaps even ask you some questions. If they do that, that's a good sign that they truly care for their pets.

- **Try buying from pet conventions and spider – related exhibitions if any**. This is where hobbyists, keepers and breeders come to buy, sell, and generally network with each other regarding their common interest in spiders. This can be a great place to find like-minded people, share your interests in a pet that may not be universally loved by everyone, and to establish great networking opportunities with breeders from whom you may buy, ask questions, and possibly even sell or trade some of your own spider species.

Selecting Bird Eating Spiders

- A healthy bird eating spider displays fluid movement when in motion and should be lively and alert.

- If the spider seems to have any curled up legs then these spiders are already ill and should be avoided.

- You also have to consider whether you would want to buy an adult, a juvenile, or a sling (baby spiders). Slings are oftentimes inexpensive but they are also more fragile, more difficult to feed, and more likely to die while molting. On the positive side though, they can be a wonderful opportunity for you to actually see the growth and development of a bird eating spider from youth to adulthood which can be a great learning experience.

- Purchasing adult bird eating spiders tends to be a bit more expensive than slings or juveniles since they're already matured and full – grown, and of course the breeder has already invested so much in them. However, the major advantage is that they do not require such delicate care compared to baby spiders, and they are generally easy to care for.

- When it comes to physical characteristics, bird eating spiders should possess a balance level of alertness and aggression since they are natural predators. Don't choose a spider that looks lethargic or doesn't react when touched by a human.

- Spiders that have unhealthy looking cream-colored splotches scattered over their body could be an indication of an infection from unclean water so stay away from those kinds of species.

- You should also check for any inconsistencies with their body parts or if there are any forms of discharge or injuries in their body.

- Try to also avoid bird eating spiders that are hunched over with their legs curled under them or if their legs are too thin for their age as this could be an indication of dehydration or other illnesses.

- Make sure that they are as large and heavy as they need to be because that's also a sign that they have properly grown. It's also helpful to ask if the spider has some history of illnesses or behavioral problems so that you'll know what kind of bird eating spider you're going to deal with as they also have their own set of personalities.

Chapter Four: Habitat Set Up for Your Bird Eating Spider

The bird eating spider is an easy to care for arachnid because they already know how to set up their own habitat and they can adapt to any kinds of surroundings, be it in the wild or in captivity. As a pet keeper though, your job is to properly set up its terrarium while factoring in the conditions the spider would actually be in if it were in its natural environment in the jungles or rainforests. It would be important to recreate temperature conditions so that it can easily be acclimated and can thrive best.

Things like choosing the right size of enclosure, the right kind of substrate, providing the fresh water and food, as well as setting up the right temperature and humidity levels can be of great help when it comes to replicating the spider's natural environment and its innate trait of burrowing underground. Designing the cage and providing climbing opportunities for your bird eating spider is also a great way to make your new pet feel at home and feel comfortable. This chapter will instruct you the step by step process on the materials you'll need, and how you can properly set up your pet's new habitat.

How to Set Up a Cage

When setting up a cage for your bird eating tarantula, what you want to achieve is something that can be good for the lifetime of your bird eating spider. Tall kinds of cages work well for tarantulas like the bird eating spiders. Although some keepers prefer to get a horizontal size cage that is quite wider and deeper. Either way, it's best that you get a taller one because it will act as an exercise opportunity for your bird eating spider since they also like to climb up and have that arboreal quality. Taller cages will also be ideal if you're trying to save up space in your house. However, you may want to get a small enclosure if your bird eating spider is still very young so that you can easily monitor its temperature and humidity. Taller and bigger cages work well for juvenile to adult spiders. Setting up the cage properly is a must so that you won't need to disturb them once they're living inside. Your goal is to set up the enclosure in such a way that you don't have to get back in there and fix things inside the tank.

Enclosure Size

You can buy a glass tank or enclosure that measures 30 x 30 x 30 cm with a secure lid to ensure that your bird eating spider doesn't escape. After acquiring the terrarium, the first thing you can do is to put a decoration or a background outside of the glass or on its back side. You can use a poster that you can buy from pet stores so in that way it can look nicer and can blend in at your house like a display. You can just easily tape it up on the back part of the glass – the side where you'd put against the wall.

Substrate

When it comes to the substrate, you can buy an orchid bark. It's a wood chip kind of substrate that's easy to clean, use, and also quite inexpensive compared to other types of bedding. After pouring in about 2 inches thick of bedding, you can add some Eco Earth bedding for humidity purposes.

The orchid bark tends to be a bit dry so adding a coconut bedding will put a little bit of extra moisture and make it possible for your pet spider to have the right kind of temperature. It will also help hold humidity inside the cage which can be great in maintaining the right environmental condition. After pouring it all in, you can start mixing them up, and ensure that the coconut bedding or Eco Earth is properly distributed with the orchid bark substrate to form a nice layer of substrate inside the cage.

Cage Furnishings

Keep in mind that bird eating spiders loves to hide in burrows or set up their web in between things. When setting up ornaments inside the cage, you can opt to buy a piece of sandblasted grapewood that resembles a log. You can set it up in away where you can see your pet bird eating spider; you can do that by simply putting the grapewood against the glass so that you can actually see how they'll build up their webs. However, the flipside to that is that most tarantulas especially the bird eating spiders want to hide in places where its dark, and putting the log against the glass may not be where your spider will hang out often since it can sense light, it may tend to hide out in the back of the cage or a place that's not too bright.

You can also choose to buy a large cork flat with like a hollow space in it, and just put it against the side of the glass where you taped the background, so that your pet can choose to set up the webs or nest in a much darker area. After doing that, you can set up the heat pad at the side of the glass or at the back of your background poster so that your pet can have the option of basking in it. Most tarantulas come out and sit on the warmer area.

Fake Plants

You can buy decorate your cage and also put fake plants inside it. You can buy a plant that looks real but something that will hold up in a cage even if it's submerged in there. You can also keep it clean once you do your spot cleaning.

Heat Pads

Make sure that you put it on a thermostat or a dimmer so that you can dial it down because it can get a bit too hot for most tarantula species. What usually happens when you set up a heat pad is that your bird eating tarantula will come out and stay in the place where the heat pad is located to keep themselves warm. You can also opt to buy radiant heat panels if you have more than one pet tarantulas or bird eating spiders. You can easily mount it on the top of the cage, and you'll see that your pets will come out to bask in the heat and get warm.

Thermometers

You should buy a thermometer to easily gauge or monitor the cage temperature and to know if the heat pad is properly set up. You can buy different kinds of thermometers in pet shops that you can easily stick at the back of the cage. Just stick it near the heat pad so that you can monitor it and prevent burning your tarantula's feet.

Temperature

You can keep the cage at 75 to 78 degrees Fahrenheit. You can also keep the cage in a cooler area in your house but make sure that you've provided them with a heated area to go. The heated areas can be turn up to 82 to 85 degrees.

Humidity

What you want to achieve is to mimic the humidity level of the wild inside the cage, and you can do that by providing them with a nice and humid cage. What you can do is to add Sphagnum moss; you can just set it up anywhere in the cage best if it's away from its main burrow area or perhaps on the sides of the cage. This way you can get the moss wet without necessarily destroying its web. The ideal humidity level is between 60 and 75%.

Humidity levels can be increased by lightly spraying water in its captive environment. Should humidity levels increase too much, just try to even out the situation by leaving out any introduction of water to the space for a few days until the humidity levels are in the right level; too much humidity encourages mold and can be fatal to your bird – eating spider.

A recommendation for budding hobbyist is a small glass fish tank which will give maximum visibility. Make sure that it comes with a fitted lid with sufficient ventilation, to keep the spider in its enclosure. A fluctuating room temperature in a warm home is best. Just keep in mind that the warmer you keep your bird eating spider, the faster its metabolism will be. They will have greater appetite, and they will grow faster, but it also means that the substrate will dry faster and they might be more prone to dehydration. Use your best judgment, and pay close attention to what seems best for your individual bird eating spiders.

Proper Husbandry for Your Bird Eating Spiders

Bird eating spiders as big as they are can still acquire certain illnesses while they are in captivity, and it's generally because of poor husbandry or insufficient diet, but most of the time it is because of unsanitary living conditions.

In order to ensure that your pet's enclosure is at its best, make sure to clean its cage thoroughly. You don't have to do it every day or every week. It's ideal that you do it at least twice a year so that you won't disturb them. However, you can still opt to do a spot cleaning at least every 2 - 3 months to give the cage a deep and thorough cleaning. You can do this by temporarily placing your spider to another holding container. Once you do, you can then remove all the contents of the tank, wash and sterilize the tank inside out, replace the substrate, clean the water dish, and sterilize all the items inside the tank before replacing them or putting them back.

You should also ensure that the temperatures and humidity levels are at the appropriate range. There are many cases of spiders dying from inappropriate levels of temperature and humidity. Molds or fungus could begin to grow in your tarantula's cage if it is too moist, this in turn could start contamination and infection on your pet. If the cage is too dry, daily misting with a substrate that holds moisture is a quick solution.

Remove any exoskeleton when it finishes molting as well as any uneaten food/ live preys or remnants of food. If you feed your bird eating spiders with live prey and your pet left them uneaten, they should be removed immediately because there is also a chance that they could attack your bird eating spider especially when they are molting.

Chapter Five: Bird Eating Spiders Handling and Behavior

When it comes to keeping tarantula species as big as the bird eating spider, it's highly recommended that you know their personalities and temperament. You would want to find out how these spiders react to certain things like human handling, and how it's going to also accept and adapt its life as a captive breed. One of the main traits of responsible spider keepers is that they tend to know everything about their pet through research and experience because this doesn't only assure a healthy and peaceful integration with the new spider into its new habitat, but it also gives the keeper an advantage of knowing what to expect when in it comes to the behavior of its new pet.

This chapter will provide you with information about the personality and behavior of bird eating spiders as well as tips on how to properly handle them, and also a general overview of their defense mechanisms.

Bird Eating Spiders Behavior

The giant bird eating tarantula has a reputation for being an ambush predator in the wild. This means that they spend their time passively hunting and waiting for their prey to fall into their web traps or walk right where they are in the position for an attack. They will easily pounce on their prey, put their fangs on it and spew venom upon the poor animal.

Whenever their burrows are raided, they tend to flee and don't build a new burrow for themselves. What they do is wander off until they find an abandoned burrow that was once inhabited by a rodent or other animals, however this often results to encounters with predators because usually abandoned burrows are also being inhabited by snakes and large centipedes.

Bird eating tarantulas are nocturnal species which means that they are active at night, and loves to stay in places that are covered in darkness. And because they are quite discreet creatures, little is known regarding their communication methods. They usually meet with other species of their own kind during the mating season. Mating usually lasts for just a few minutes because of their aggressive nature and because most females are also heavier than their male counterparts; males tend to quickly go away after mating because females see them as potential prey.

This goes to say that bird eating spiders and tarantulas in general don't like to socialize even with their own kin. They tend to live in solitary which is why most zoologists assume that these animals only have minimal level of communication between each other.

Male bird eating spiders when confronted by another male species either defend its burrow or fight for the female species. If the male can sense that the female want to mate with him, they only try to mate for a few moments then rush back to safety.

The bird eating tarantula, despite of its 'small' brains and poor eyesight, is very intelligent for an invertebrate. It is well aware of its surroundings and knows how to stand its ground when it comes face to face with larger predators.

Another proof that it is quite intelligent is when the female becomes aware that they are pregnant; what they do at least 2 weeks before laying their eggs is that they work to enlarge the space inside their burrow. According to scientists, this is evidence that these animals have some form of intelligence and is very capable of handling their surroundings and looking after themselves.

Juvenile bird eating spiders tend to stay above ground. These teenage spiders tend to choose lairs under rocks or fallen logs instead of burrowing itself underground. They also spend the majority of their time dodging predators, hunting smaller prey to dine on and during breeding season they can be found hanging around the burrows of females trying to entice one for copulation.

Tips for Handling Bird Eating Spiders

Tarantula species like bird eating spiders are really not meant to be handled. It's mostly a pet you keep for observation. They don't benefit from handling, and they really don't care if you handle them or not, don't expect them to love you back just like when you are petting your cats or dogs. Keep in mind, they're not social creatures. They shy away even from their own kind, so what makes you think you and your itsy bitsy spider can become good friends? They'll try to get away from you not because they don't like you but because they're scared that you might crush them (natural instincts in the wild), they might even try to mistake you for a predator and bite you. However, as a responsible keeper who took the commitment to care for these animals (even if they didn't really ask for it), your job is to keep them safe and provide them with everything they need – and part of the job is handling them once in a while.

Handling tarantulas like this one can provide a thrilling experience for you as the owner but again as much as possible try not to handle them because if you do that they can get stressed and cause them to be ill. Here are some tips when handling bird eating spiders:

- First of all, there's a huge possibility that you'll get bitten so if you don't want to experience being stung by a bird eating spider (it's quite painful and can make you dizzy for a few hours), you might want to get some kind of gloves on to protect you.

- Before you try to handle your pet, make sure to check its current move. The best way is to use a stick or a tong, you can slightly brush them or like use the equipment to touch their legs so that you can gauge their behavior at the moment, and perhaps let your spider know you're trying to do something.

- Once you do the "introduction," you can then slowly coax it out of the container using the brush/ tong, and place your hand near the container where it can walk right through. Be gentle to them since they are also gentle creatures.

- Another thing you can try is to slowly pick them up with your fingers and just cup them from the top. Put your fingers/ hands underneath their legs because in this way your spider is cradled, and you're not sort of smashing down on it. However, this may not apply to handling big or adult bird eating spiders as they may become threatened.

- You can also try to coax them in your hand as they are walking and just give them a little nudge on their abdomen so that he'll walk right through your hand.

- Most tarantulas don't like the feeling of human hand because it's something foreign to them, and they would want to move out as soon as possible.

- Make sure that whenever you're holding them, you keep them near the ground because they'll try to jump and get away from you. It will prevent them in falling from great heights.

- After doing that, you can then slowly place them back inside their cage or enclosure the same way you coax them out. Remember, try to be as gentle as possible because these creatures are very fragile and a bit of pressure can break them.

Chapter Six: Feeding Your Bird Eating Spiders

When feeding these bird eating spiders, what most breeders do is to pick a day of the week, and just stick to that schedule. Don't worry about skipping a day or two because these tarantulas have very slow metabolism which means that they can usually withstand a couple of days without eating but of course it's better to stick in your basic routine. Do keep in mind that these creatures are cannibals too so better not leave another spider around or else they'll fight to the death until one of them devour the other.

This chapter will provide you with a wealth of information about how to properly feed your bird eating spider, what to feed them, the tools to use when feeding them, and also some feeding tips. Providing them with the right amount of nutrition will keep them strong and healthy against diseases, and also make them live a long life.

Tools to Use When Feeding Bird Eating Spiders

There are some basic things that you're going to need in order to properly feed your bird eating spider.

Tweezers/ Tongs

You should have a pair of bent nose tweezers that you can use for your sling spiders. This is a great tool because you can easily control it and it's also small which is perfect for handling tiny insects like roaches that you need later on. You can also use a larger set of tongs that you can use for your bird eating spider once they get fully grown or use it to feed larger insects.

Some breeders also use long tweezers for their aggressive eaters, if in case you have an aggressive bird eating spider, this will keep your hands safe so that your spider won't mistake your hands for food.

Paint Brush

You can keep a paint brush around just so you can coax your pet if ever he/she tries to escape. The bristles on the soft brush tends to not irritate or scare off your spider, which is why it's a perfect handy dandy tool to keep them under controlled without threatening them. If you use your tongs or tweezers or things that are hard like metal tools, it usually causes them to panic and be in an attack mode.

Catch Cup

You can use this if ever your spider tries to escape during feeding time. Most spiders tend to stay inside their enclosure where it is safe, but there could be instances where they will try to flee away, so that's the reason why you need to have a catch cup around just in case.

Squeeze Bottles

Never use large spray bottles because it tends to spook the spider and will cause them to ball up. What you can use is a scientific squeeze bottle that you can buy from pet stores, sport centers or Amazon and other online shops. The reason for this is that the squeeze bottles are very precise in putting in the water exactly where you want it, and also minimize the risk of spraying too much on your spider. The squeeze bottles have hoses that are very precise in squirting water. Spray bottles can be a major problem especially when you're dealing with slings or baby spiders because they tend to be more skittish and they'll try to escape or hide away inside their cave and may take a long while before they come out.

How to Feed Your Bird Eating Spiders

When it comes to feeding, most keepers and breeders worry about their pets not eating or not growing but you have to keep mind that these pets will naturally just take care of themselves and they'll eventually eat the food you give them.

Some owners feed their sling pets with fruit flies but some don't like that because these flies tend to be all over the place or because they thought that their pet baby spiders may not be able to find them but nothing could be farther from the truth as most keepers find that after putting a couple of flies in the enclosure, the spiders seem to know or they seem to sense where this flies are no matter how small they may be, and just easily gobble them up.

Baby spiders tend to grow quite rapidly in just a matter of weeks, they'll molt and then they'll double in size up until a certain point where they can start taking care of themselves and start taking down larger preys. Once they reach that point, you can then give them small size roaches or other small size insects.

What you can do is just drop it inside their enclosure using your tongs or small tweezers right in the spot where your spider is located so that you can later check back on it. If the flies or insects are gone then you'll know that your spider have already eaten them. If the prey is still there, it's better if you just pull it out and offer a fresh roach or insect.

If you notice your spider refusing to eat, it could mean that they are getting ready to molt. You don't need to worry too much about it but just keep an eye and monitor him from time to time. Generally, they'll find their prey and eat it when they feel like doing so.

It's pretty much the same when feeding juvenile or adult bird eating spiders. You can just slowly put in larger preys like earthworms, roaches, insects that are gut loaded with necessary nutrients, and you can do that with your tongs. Once you've successfully placed it in, and you've seen your spider devour it with its mighty fangs, you can then start misting water with it to keep the substrate moist. You can use the squeeze bottle to pour in a bit of water in there.

You shouldn't try to put a small water dish in the enclosure especially if they're still young and small because they can drown in it, though some keepers use shallow water dishes like bottle caps, which can be doable. They usually get hydrated through the substrate or the walls of their enclosure/ container since the humidity should be a bit higher when you're housing baby spiders otherwise they'll dry out very quickly.

Feeding them could be a rewarding experience. Just keep in mind that if they don't take the food, you have to understand that they probably just finished molting that's why they're not ready to take down food; it's the same thing if they're preparing for their molting season because they wouldn't want to take in live preys. Keep in mind to never leave any live prey when they're preparing to molt as it could end up being catastrophic for your pet and you because you might come back to see that your pet has been eaten or missing a leg or two due to the live prey devouring them. So just be careful with that and always monitor your bird eating spider whenever you're feeding them.

Chapter Seven: Breeding Your Bird Eating Spiders

There are many varieties of spider species being discovered by zoologists and hobbyists but it's very important to note that before you decide to become a breeder, you're well aware of the conservation status of these species as some are already endangered. Breeding spiders is quite difficult for first timers, which is why it's wise that you ask help from veteran breeders if you really wanted to learn the process and take the endeavor of caring for these pets and their offspring. There is a science to the method of mating and breeding spiders which should be taken in consideration.

This chapter will guide you in learning about how to properly breed this bird eating spiders. However, if you're really serious about this and if you want to become a reputable spider breeder, then you better keep studying and learn as much as you can with regards successful pairing and breeding. The best way to learn is to experience and try it for yourself with the help of legit breeders and veteran spider hobbyists.

Sexing Bird Eating Spiders

What you want to do is put them down on the ground or in a flat surface where they won't hurt themselves if they fall or jump out of the enclosure. During mating season the male bird eating spiders would purposely seek out female spiders that have hidden themselves in their deep burrows. The males would then entice the female out to mate at the entrance of the females burrow. Usually male spiders begin a display of courtship by raising its abdomen or the bulky area of their body while lowering the front of its body. It would shake its pedipalps as it moves back and forth. An interested female will accept its advances willingly while an unreceptive one will viciously attack or will try to prey on the male.

When the male bird eating spider is finished or if ever he survived the ordeal, the successful male, would hold back the fangs of the female with its legs and then they have the tendency to escape and run for their lives. They'll immediately get out of the cage and flee away because the females could attack them and eat them, so you just have to let the males do that. Never close the cage or the container where they'll mate so that the males can easily escape otherwise they have a big chance of getting eaten after the mating process - and they most likely will since most females are larger and heavier than male bird eating spiders.

Before breeding a female, make sure that she is well fed; otherwise your male spider will become their dinner. There are many breeders who suggest that it's better if you put the female into the male's enclosure because then the female will not think about food or eating the male since it's in a new environment, and it could make her slightly less aggressive. The other way around is to put the male or introduce the male spider to the female's lair, so just try and see how they'll both react to one another.

You can also put them in their own open containers and just get it near each other so that they can have a sense of mating. Or you can also use the catch cup to introduce the male to the opposite end of the enclosure where the female is.

As soon as the male and female successfully mount one another, you'll see an instant response. Usually, the male will stop walking because the male will sense that a female is around through its sensory hairs, mouth or pheromones

When to Breed Tarantulas

Tarantulas are more active at night; male bird eating spiders usually seek out females at night since they are nocturnal creatures so don't expect them to mate during the day like what other species do. This is because in the wild, these animals are a lot more secure at night from potential predators than day are in the day.

Female bird eating spiders have heat cycles so they usually accept a male during their heat cycle but not before the molting season. If you're going to breed them in captivity, make sure that you don't put in a female bird eating spider with a male spider that's currently molting because this can be dangerous since the molting stage is where all spiders are vulnerable to predation because they are defenseless at this stage. Female bird eating spiders tend to eat them right after mating. You can give the spiders around 2 or 3 weeks after the final molting period so that the males can properly produce a sperm web, after that they can mate with one another.

Before you do the breeding, make sure to select healthy tarantulas as unhealthy specimens will yield unhealthy offspring. Identify that the spiders being paired are sexually mature and capable of breeding and production. A healthy male should be placed in the terrarium of an equally healthy female. They should be observed to make sure the female does not inflict harm to the male.

Some breeders choose to mate a female with two healthy males to ensure absolute mating success. Keep in mind that this procedure will take up your time which is why if you're not serious about it, then maybe it's not a wise idea to push through, otherwise you would just stress your pets out.

Tools to Use When Breeding

Make sure that all of the things you're going to use as aid in the mating or breeding process are clean. Here are some things you can use:

- **Catch cup:** You can use this to transfer your bird eating spiders back to their enclosure after mating.

- **Cardboard cut outs:** You can use this as a shield if the female spider is not responsive to the breeding process.

- **Chopstick or something similar:** You can put the chopstick in front of the female if ever she is being receptive or aggressive towards the male. It can function as an obstacle to the female's legs if ever it's showing signs of aggression towards the male spiders. If ever they both act normally and gets into the mating position where they are trying to both mount each other, then you can slowly lift up the chopstick from the female's legs. Most tarantulas have excellent chemical reception, they know if there are other spiders around who wanted to mate them.

Mating Rituals

The mating ritual involves the male drumming its pedipalps (or legs) and the female drums back, or he'll do a periodic tapping. If that's not how your spiders respond to one another, you can use the chopstick to get some silk from the females in its pedipalps, and then let the male sort of sniff it or get it into its mouth so that there can be some kind of reaction and excite the male to get them both into the mood. You can also get the male's silk in its pedipalps and take it to the female so that they're both aware that there's an opposite sex nearby and can get them to mate one another.

While the mating is going on, it's important to just monitor them from afar and not make any sudden moves or noises or breathe into them; tarantulas gets turned off when humans breathe into them for some reason, so just monitor them and pick them up once the mating is over. It will usually just take a few minutes. You'll know when it's done, if the male is already trying to run away from the female.

Breeding Basics for Bird Eating Spiders

- Just a few days or weeks after mating successfully, the females would lay about fifty eggs into its sac that measures about three centimeters in diameter. This sac will be stored in a burrow and the eggs are protected by a sturdy cover of silk webbing. The mother will also try to expand the burrow if need be

- The baby bird eating spiders will experience their first molt while they are in the sac. They then leave the sac and molt a second time before leaving the safety of the burrow to live out in the wild.

- Bird eating spiders like most tarantulas mate at over a specific season of the year given that it has completed its molting process. The molting of these spiders usually occurs once a year; every 5 years for male spiders, and a continuous process for females, throughout its life time.

Chapter Eight: Raising Bird Eating Slings

Raising baby bird eating spiders is quite easy if you've already taken care of a couple of spiders. However, slings are delicate creatures because they are still young and very fragile at this point which is why handling them with care is very important. It's also necessary to start raising them right by maintaining proper husbandry practices, providing them with nutritious foods, and also making sure that they are always hydrated and have the right environmental conditions. This chapter will enlighten you with all the things you need when it comes to raising slings.

Enclosures

When it comes to choosing an enclosure for your baby bird eating spiders, what you can do is buy a plastic cup or a deli cup that's about medium to large in size (you can buy it a 32 oz. cup or a 16 oz. cup). You can easily secure it with the cup cover but make sure that it is well ventilated otherwise your sling will dry out. You can do that by poking holes into the sides of the cup using equipment that you can buy at Amazon. The more ventilation or holes in the cup, the better. If ever you punched in a large hole, what you can do is to just take out a tape and seal the hole up so that your little spider won't be able to escape.

Aside from cheap deli cups, you can also try to house your slings in glass boxes because they're very easy to open up and can make feeding or misting easier. You can also try buying containers that's shape like a drum or a capsule like bottle that you can easily punch holes in for ventilation. These are all very cheap and also very durable until your slings grow in size.

Tiny Cork Bars and Other Accessories

You can buy small cork bars or logs for decoration, or you can just pick up a wood and chop it off into small pieces that can fit inside your sling's enclosure. This can work well especially for terrestrial species like the bird eating spiders.

You can also add in small plastic leaves as well as shallow water dishes like bottle caps that you can take from bottles.

Substrate

Sphagnum moss is a must so that your sling will have bedding that can handle moisture. It's also great for burrowing. You should also provide top soil or other kinds of substrate like coco fiber, peat or a mixture of all of these kinds as long as they can hold moisture because it's very important to not let your pet get dehydrated.

How to Set Up the Enclosure

Step #1: Take out the deli cup and put the substrate in. Once you pour it out, make sure that you pat down the soil around the enclosure. After doing that, you can then use a spray or squeeze bottle to mist the soil and keep it moisted. Once you've done that, you can then add a little more dry soil on the top of the wet soil, and just simply pat down the soil.

Step #2: You can now put the decorations like the mini cork bar and the plastic leaves or plants. You can start digging up a starter burrow so that your pet can easily web it up.

Step #3: Once you've done that, you can add the sphagnum moss on one side of the enclosure, and make sure to spray a bit of water in it to keep the moisture in. Then you can add the bottle caps which will function as a water bowl. You don't have to fill it up especially if you think that your spider will drown in it but since bird eating spiders are naturally a large species, you won't have a problem with that.

Feeding Slings

Feeding spiders or slings for this matter seems like an easy thing to do because you have your hungry pet, you put in the prey, and they eat it, they molt, they grow and everything's fine. Unfortunately, it doesn't always go that way. Part of the problem is that most keepers have a hard time knowing what kind of food to feed their slings because these creatures can be very tiny and quite difficult for the keeper to find a prey that will suit the size of their pet.

Crickets

You can feed them with small to medium size crickets. Crickets are very easy to find in pet stores. They also come in many sizes, the y can be bought in small amount, and they're perfect for young bird eating spiders.

Mealworms

You can also feed your pet with mealworms which is another easy feeder to find in pet stores. However, you can't buy them in small amounts, but you can put them in the fridge and just stock it up. They also come in different sizes, and they're also very inexpensive and easy to feed to young and juvenile tarantulas.

B. Laterals

These creatures may be quite difficult to find in your local pet stores, and you may also need to buy them in large quantity but they come in convenient sizes but they can be invasive so make sure that they're always sealed up.

Roaches

Another feeder that's hard to find and also invasive but they're also great meals to feed to your young bird eating spider. You may need to also buy them in large quantities or raise your own if ever you have a collection of spiders.

Feeding Reminders

- When it comes to the size, the general rule of thumb is to not feed prey items that are longer than your bird eating spider's body. For slings, smaller is better because they can also be intimidated by larger prey items.

- If ever your tarantula is not interested for some reason (unless they're molting), you may try to start off with something small preys. You can also try feeding them pre – killed items or chopping the feeders into bite size pieces if they don't feel like eating a live prey.

Hydration

Tarantulas especially slings are very vulnerable to dehydration since they don't have a waxy coating that can trap in the moisture which is why it's important to keep them hydrated and also give them options like water bowls. Here are some techniques you can try to ensuring that your pet is well hydrated:

- Aside from bottle caps, you can use other things like shallow pods or even Lego blocks, the important thing is you find something that works for you and something that's also easy to pluck out and replace if ever it gets old or too dirty. You can just fill it up with the spray, and fill them up every time you feed your slings or just keep the water dish full from time to time.

- What you can do when you're setting up the enclosure is to make a furrow using a stick or a pencil and start it off so that the underground area of the substrate can also be misted. Make sure that the bottom part of the enclosure stays moist by spraying water periodically.

- Having furrows on the side makes it much easier to add water. The top layer of the substrate can dry up a bit but make sure that the bottom layer is moist so that your sling can get hydrated. You can also use a dropper and just drop water on the furrows located at the side of the cage. Make sure though that you don't put it in where the tarantula is currently burrowed in otherwise they could drown. You also want to make sure that you don't put in too much water in a way that it would fill up your sling's burrow.

- You should also try misting the sides of the enclosure around night time since they are nocturnal creatures. They will come out at night and they can get hydrated. If you mist the enclosure in the morning and your spider is in its burrow, the water will just easily evaporate and your pet wouldn't be able to drink it. Another very important reminder is to ensure that you avoid over spraying especially if you live in a place where it's already humid.

Maintenance

Tarantulas are very neat animals, which is why husbandry wouldn't be a huge problem. Here are some tips when cleaning up the cage or enclosure of your slings:

- Take out any molts after they have it. If you can't get to the molt because it's located in a burrow, don't worry about it. Molt residues are not harmful to your pets even if you leave them there. It also doesn't attract pests or fungus. Leave it in if it's out of reach because your spider can also use it when creating another burrow. Use your tongs or tweezers when picking a molt out.

- For sling enclosures, you can do a routine maintenance at least 2x a week. For juvenile spiders, once a week is enough.

- You can also try to clean up the remnants of the prey and take it out using the tongs. If you can't find it or it's buried somewhere, just leave it in because usually only little parts are left behind.

- You don't necessarily need to change the substrate; you can actually leave it in there until your pet outgrows the enclosure.

- If ever the enclosure has molds, make sure to remove it or clean it up and put in substrate around it. You can let the cage dry up a bit, and ensure that you improve the ventilation inside to prevent fungus growth.

Temperature and Humidity

When raising slings, you don't want to fixate on the individual temperatures inside the enclosures nor do you want to become obsessed with false ideal temperatures that you read out of care sheets online. The bottom line is, if you're comfortable in the room temperature, then your tarantulas are fine. Temperatures higher than 90 degrees are potentially harmful for spiders, so try to keep it around 60 degrees. Another tip is that cooler temperatures may lead to slower metabolism and slower growth though this is not entirely bad for a sling. Most slings will do well especially if the temperature is around 68 and 84 degrees Fahrenheit. Temperature below 68 for short stretches also doesn't harm most tarantula species.

Chapter Nine: The Spider Molting Process

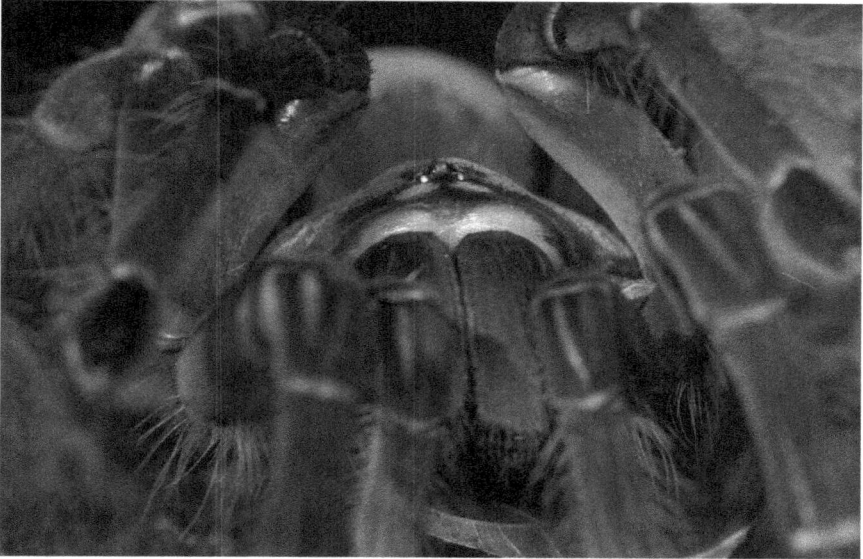

The molting process is a spider's natural process of growing but it's the part that makes new keepers (and even experienced ones) freaks out but just recognize that it's a very natural process of these creatures. Your job as a responsible keeper is to ensure that you aid them during this molting process because there are certain requirements that you need to keep in mind like not offering them any food or live prey, keeping them hydrated and moisturized, not touching them or disturbing them during the whole process as this is the point where they are very vulnerable. Molting will happen to your pet every now and then but with experience you'll easily get used to it.

Stages of Molting

Intermolt

This is the stage where the bird eating spider or tarantulas in general are still eating normally anytime your feed and behaving normally as this is part of the growing process. This is where your pet is doing their usual routines and still quite active. You'll also notice that the abdomen skin of the spider is pale which is in its normal shade. This is also the stage that doesn't make tarantula keepers panic or stressed out. However, simultaneously your spider is at a point where it's developing a new exoskeleton beneath its old exoskeleton. This is how they grow, and as these exoskeleton starts to develop, eventually the spider will eat enough, its body will then send out hormone signals that tells the spider that's it's time to stop eating. This is when you'll start to see some behavioral changes; your spider may seem lethargic or secretive, and they will not eat at all.

Proecdysis

This is the next stage of the molting process. This is when the molt is imminent. The spider's body will start pumping fluids in the 2 sets of its exoskeletons to get the body ready to molt. This is the point where your bird eating spider is ready to fully undergo through the molting process. You'll notice that the skin will become dark especially its abdominal area, and you may also see fluids leaking from its joints. They may also start to lay down in molting mats.

Ecdysis

This is the molting proper. It is the part where the tarantula will expand itself to pop its limbs and work its way out of the molt. This process can take many hours to at least 1 day depending on the current size of your bird eating spider. This is also the point where your pet is very vulnerable, you shouldn't touch or disturb them.

Postecdysis

This is the stage where the bird eating spider is already folding its new exoskeleton. You'll see the skin filling out and hardening, you'll also see it stretching. The fangs at this point is delicately soft that's why it won't be able to eat. You should wait for at least a few days to a couple of weeks before you offer them food. It's also important to keep in mind that at this stage, your spider can lose a lot of its moisture and can get dehydrated whenever they undergo through this process, so make sure that its enclosure or substrate is moist and well hydrated.

Signs of Molting

Sign #1: Your pet stops eating

Whatever age your spider may be, when your pet suddenly stops eating or isn't showing any interest in food like they'll just walk around the prey, not care about it, or even just bite it and leave the prey alone then chances are that they are in pre – molt.

Sign #2: Your pet will develop a large and dark or shiny abdomen

If you have slings, you'll see that their abdomens will get really bulky and also shiny. You may also see a dark spot in the back of the abdomen. The spider will put on more size and the abdomen will start to have thick hairs. It will also have a bruise appearance on its abdomen. You'll also see a purple colored shade in it that used to be in a fleshy tone when they're not molting. If the abdomen is plump, blowing up, shiny or the once fleshy tone turns dark, then that means your pet is in pre – molt.

Sign #3: Your pet will become more lethargic

You can expect your pet to become very laid back, slow or less energetic. This applies also to some tarantula species that doesn't appear to be changing in color or showing physical signs. You can check their behavior and eating patterns to know if they're undergoing the molting process. If they are active or if your spider is aggressive before then suddenly it's not then that's a sign to watch out for.

Sign #4: Your pet will bury itself underground

Bird eating spiders will dig up and try to bury themselves in burrows. They might also blocked out the entrance in their burrows by webbing it as this is their way of keeping themselves protected from possible intruders. Never dig them up or put a prey insider their burrows or wherever they buried themselves in. This is their way of not letting other creatures and you from disturbing themselves while experiencing molting.

Sign #5: Your pet will lay down a molting mat

You'll notice that if the molting period is about to come, your pet will set up their molting mats; this is a web mat for tarantulas that are usually set up on the ground or on the sides of the glass enclosure. When you see your pet lying down on its back then that means the molting process is about to take place. At this point you shouldn't touch your pet or flip it over. Just let it run its course and go through the whole processed undisturbed. The best thing you can do is to just observe them and monitor them.

Chapter 10: Summary and Care Sheet

This chapter contains the summary of the book and all the important things you need to keep in mind when it comes to keeping bird eating tarantulas. Always remember that proper husbandry and feeding will go a long way in your pet's longevity. As a responsible keeper, it's your job to ensure that they're well provided and taken care of. You don't need to always keep an eye out on these creatures unlike other house pets like cats or dogs, you don't even need to clean up after them, and they can be totally left on their own devises as long as you keep them secure and safe.

That being said though, you still have to give them the attention that they need. Have fun!

Physical Features

- Bird eating spiders are the biggest and heaviest spider species in the world with an average weight of 170 grams (6 oz).

- The giant bird eating spiders have many sensitive hairs on all of its 8 legs. They are arachnid creatures that don't have any inner skeleton structure or a backbone. They have exoskeleton which can be described as a hard outer covering or an outer skeletal framework.

- The bird eating spider is a ground dwelling spiders which are also adept climbers. Their legs are equip with suction - like cups able to produce a substance which allows them to climb any sort of surface with ease, with no need for web weaving.

- The giant bird eating spider will tend to shed its outer skeletal structure every now and then (a process called molting), so that it can grow and create a new set of exoskeleton. Molting allows spiders to grow and also repair its broken legs. It's regeneration ability. Once the new limb is formed, it usually appears small and underdeveloped at first but as time goes by, it will slowly increase in size and also gain mass after each molting season until it reaches its normal size.

- Its fangs measures about 2 ½ inches which is equal to the length of a cheetah's claws, this is why penetrating a human skin can be very easy. The venom from their fangs can be fatal to most animals, and can cause nausea, vomiting, and severe pain to humans.

Behavioral Characteristics

- Giant bird eating spiders usually create a hissing sound whenever it feels threatened, and it is done by rubbing its legs very rapidly which then produces the miniature missile like spiky hairs that can protect him from predators.

- When it comes to defense mechanisms, the first line of defense for the bird eating spider is to retreat or withdraw from a potential predator or attacker. It will also produce a hissing sound by rubbing rows of tiny spines or hair – like spins around their hind legs or near the bulky area of their body. This is where the hissing sound comes from not in its mouth.

- When it comes to feeding; in the wild bird eating spiders are known to be general eaters with relatively healthy appetites. In captivity, a bird eating spider may be fed pinkies or other insects like grasshoppers, crickets, earthworms, and even cockroaches to name a few.

- Molting also signals that the spider is preparing itself for breeding. The period of molting is extremely stressful to a tarantula species like the bird eating spider, which is why during this period, they should not be disturbed nor should they be offered food like a live prey as they may not be in their best condition to chomp down another animal.

Taxonomy: Kingdom Animalia, Phylum Arthropoda, Class Arachnida, Order Araneae, Family Theraphosidae, Genus Theraphosa, Species Blondi.

Distribution: These spiders range in rainforests and wild jungles in southern America, northern Australia, northern Brazil, Venezuela, Guyana, and French Guiana

Habitat: hey inhabit burrows left by rodents/ rats, and build their sets of webs and trip – like wires in it.

Conservation and Licensing

- The population of these animals is relatively stable but from time to time it's experiencing a constant threat to its survival, this is because many bird eating spiders are being captured for illegal pet trade.

- If you plan on acquiring one or more of these bird eating spiders, then you should check with your local animal or pet organization to determine if owning one would need licensure in your state or place of residence. Even if there are no state laws regarding pet spiders, it is highly advised that you check in your town or village if there are any rules because these might provide further regulations regarding pet spiders even when state law otherwise allows it.

Keeping Bird Eating Spiders as Pets

- If you wanted to keep more than one or even just one, then you should be physically and financially prepared to care for each one of these spiders.

- You must have sufficient space to house each one of the spiders, and you should be financially prepared and able to support and provide for all their needs.
- Ideally, you should house your pets in separate encasements to avoid attacks, fights and the potential to prey on one another.

- You as a keeper should also ensure that you monitor all of them and provide them with enough attention in terms of food and husbandry.

- If you really are aiming to keep more than one bird eating spider or any kind of spider for that matter, make sure you have assigned specific enclosures for each of them. Never attempt a communal setup unless you have done extensive research and have several years of experience in keeping and caring for these kinds of pet.

- A multi species terrarium housing two or more arachnid or bird eating spiders will have to be quite large to accommodate each of the creatures which are separated by individual enclosures.

- Keep in mind that tarantulas are cannibals, and if you decide to house your pet with other species there will surely fight to the death.

- It's also best to quarantine your pet especially if you didn't acquire it from a reputable breeder as it can come directly from the wild. Testing and treating each animal for the presence of parasite and/or harmful pathogens will be very costly.

Reminders When Choosing Where to Buy

Search online and read the reviews. Reading testimonials of people who have already bought tarantulas from specific breeders is a must so that you have an idea of the type of breeder/s you'll be dealing with

Check various forums or join groups online. Thanks to the internet, you can now get recommendations from people about where to buy and not to buy. Ask for recommendations and from there do your own comparison.

See it for yourself! Once you have prospective breeder, it's best to come to their place or breeding facility if any so that you'll have an idea of how these spiders were raised.

Ask away! Don't hesitate to ask questions especially the important ones. If they are a reputable and passionate breeder, they'll understand your inquisitive nature.

Try buying from pet conventions and spider – related exhibitions if any. This is where hobbyists, keepers and breeders come to buy, sell, and generally network with each other regarding their common interest in spiders.

Selecting a Healthy Spider

- If the spider seems to have any curled up legs then these spiders are already ill and should be avoided.

- When it comes to physical characteristics, bird eating spiders should possess a balance level of alertness and aggression since they are natural predators. Don't choose a spider that looks lethargic or doesn't react when touched by a human.

- Spiders that have unhealthy looking cream-colored splotches scattered over their body could be an indication of an infection from unclean water so stay away from those kinds of species.

- You should also check for any inconsistencies with their body parts or if there are any forms of discharge or injuries in their body.

- Make sure that they are as large and heavy as they need to be because that's also a sign that they have properly grown.

Housing Bird Eating Tarantulas

Enclosure Size: You can buy a glass tank or enclosure that measures 30 x 30 x 30 cm with a secure lid to ensure that your bird eating spider doesn't escape.

Substrate: When it comes to the substrate, you can buy an orchid bark. It's a wood chip kind of substrate that's easy to clean, use, and also quite inexpensive compared to other types of bedding. After pouring in about 2 inches thick of bedding, you can add some Eco Earth bedding for humidity purposes.

Cage Furnishings: When setting up ornaments inside the cage, you can opt to buy a piece of sandblasted grapewood that resembles a log. You can also choose to buy a large cork flat with like a hollow space in it so that your pet can choose to set up the webs or nest in a much darker area.

Heat Pads: Make sure that you put it on a thermostat or a dimmer so that you can dial it down because it can get a bit too hot for most tarantula species.

Thermometers: You should buy a thermometer to easily gauge or monitor the cage temperature and to know if the heat pad is properly set up.

Temperature: You can keep the cage at 75 to 78 degrees Fahrenheit.

Humidity: The ideal humidity level is between 60 and 75%.

Proper Husbandry for Your Bird Eating Spiders

- It's ideal that you do it at least twice a year so that you won't disturb them. However, you can still opt to do a spot cleaning at least every 2 - 3 months to give the cage a deep and thorough cleaning.

- Make sure to remove all the contents of the tank, wash and sterilize the tank inside out, replace the substrate, clean the water dish, and sterilize all the items inside the tank before replacing them or putting them back

- Remove any exoskeleton when it finishes molting as well as any uneaten food/ live preys or remnants of food. If you feed your bird eating spiders with live prey and your pet left them uneaten.

Bird Eating Spiders Behavior

- The giant bird eating tarantula has a reputation for being an ambush predator in the wild. This means that they spend their time passively hunting and waiting for their prey to fall into their web traps or walk right where they are in the position for an attack.

- Whenever their burrows are raided, they tend to flee and don't build a new burrow for themselves.

- Bird eating tarantulas are nocturnal species which means that they are active at night, and loves to stay in places that are covered in darkness

- Bird eating spiders and tarantulas in general don't like to socialize even with their own kin.

- Male bird eating spiders when confronted by another male species either defend its burrow or fight for the female species.

- Juvenile bird eating spiders tend to stay above ground. These teenage spiders tend to choose lairs under rocks or fallen logs instead of burrowing itself underground.

Handling Tips

- Before you try to handle your pet, make sure to check its current move. The best way is to use a stick or a tong, you can slightly brush them or like use the equipment to touch their legs so that you can gauge their behavior at the moment, and perhaps let your spider know you're trying to do something.

- Once you do the "introduction," you can then slowly coax it out of the container using the brush/ tong, and place your hand near the container where it can walk right through. Be gentle to them since they are also gentle creatures.

- Another thing you can try is to slowly pick them up with your fingers and just cup them from the top. Put your fingers/ hands underneath their legs because in this way your spider is cradled, and you're not sort of smashing down on it. However, this may not apply to handling big or adult bird eating spiders as they may become threatened.

- You can also try to coax them in your hand as they are walking and just give them a little nudge on their abdomen so that he'll walk right through your hand.

Tools to Use When Feeding Bird Eating Spiders

Tweezers/ Tongs: This is a great tool because you can easily control it and it's also small which is perfect for handling tiny insects like roaches that you need later on.

Paint Brush: The bristles on the soft brush tends to not irritate or scare off your spider, which is why it's a perfect handy dandy tool to keep them under controlled without threatening them.

Catch Cup: You can use this if ever your spider tries to escape during feeding time.

Squeeze Bottles: Squeeze bottles are very precise in putting in the water exactly where you want it, and also minimize the risk of spraying too much on your spider. The squeeze bottles have hoses that are very precise in squirting water.

Feeding Tips

- When feeding them what you can do is to drop the food inside their enclosure using your tongs or small tweezers right in the spot where your spider is located so that you can later check back on it

- If the prey is still there, it's better if you just pull it out and offer a fresh roach or insect. If you notice your spider refusing to eat, it could mean that they are getting ready to molt.

- You can just slowly put in larger preys like earthworms, roaches, insects that are gut loaded with necessary nutrients, and you can do that with your tongs.

- Once you've successfully placed it in, and you've seen your spider devour it with its mighty fangs, you can

then start misting water with it to keep the substrate
moist.

- Be careful with that and always monitor your bird
  eating spider whenever you're feeding them

Breeding Basics for Bird Eating Spiders

- Just a few days or weeks after mating successfully,
  the females would lay about fifty eggs into its sac that
  measures about three centimeters in diameter. This
  sac will be stored in a burrow and the eggs are
  protected by a sturdy cover of silk webbing. The
  mother will also try to expand the burrow if need be

- The baby bird eating spiders will experience their first
  molt while they are in the sac. They then leave the sac
  and molt a second time before leaving the safety of
  the burrow to live out in the wild.

- Bird eating spiders like most tarantulas mate at over a
  specific season of the year given that it has completed
  its molting process. The molting of these spiders

usually occurs once a year; every 5 years for male spiders, and a continuous process for females, throughout its life time.

Raising Bird Eating Slings

Enclosures: When it comes to choosing an enclosure for your baby bird eating spiders, what you can do is buy a plastic cup or a deli cup that's about medium to large in size (you can buy it a 32 oz. cup or a 16 oz. cup).

Tiny Cork Bars and Other Accessories: You can buy small cork bars or logs for decoration, or you can just pick up a wood and chop it off into small pieces that can fit inside your sling's enclosure.

Substrate: Sphagnum moss is a must so that your sling will have bedding that can handle moisture. It's also great for burrowing.

Feeder Prey for Slings

Crickets: You can feed them with small to medium size crickets.

Mealworms: You can also feed your pet with mealworms which is another easy feeder to find in pet stores. However, you can't buy them in small amounts, but you can put them in the fridge and just stock it up.

B. Laterals: These creatures may be quite difficult to find in your local pet stores, and you may also need to buy them in large quantity.

Roaches: Another feeder that's hard to find and also invasive but they're also great meals to feed to your young bird eating spider.

Husbandry Tips

- When it comes to hydrating them, you can use things like shallow pods or bottle caps. The important thing is you find something that works for you and something that's also easy to pluck out and replace if ever it gets old or too dirty. You can just fill it up with the spray, and fill them up every time you feed your slings or just keep the water dish full from time to time.

- What you can do when you're setting up the enclosure is to make a furrow. Make sure that the bottom part of the enclosure stays moist by spraying water periodically.

- Make sure though that you don't put it in where the tarantula is currently burrowed in otherwise they could drown. You also want to make sure that you don't put in too much water in a way that it would fill up your sling's burrow.

- You should also try misting the sides of the enclosure around night time since they are nocturnal creatures.

- Another very important reminder is to ensure that you avoid over spraying especially if you live in a place where it's already humid.

- Take out any molts after they have it. Use your tongs or tweezers when picking a molt out. If you can't reach it, then just leave it in. Molt residues are not harmful to your pets even if you leave them there. It also doesn't attract pests or fungus.

- For sling enclosures, you can do a routine maintenance at least 2x a week. For juvenile spiders, once a week is enough.

- You can also try to clean up the remnants of the prey and take it out using the tongs.

- If ever the enclosure has molds, make sure to remove it or clean it up and put in substrate around it.

Temperatures

- Most slings will do well especially if the temperature is around 68 and 84 degrees Fahrenheit. Temperature below 68 for short stretches also doesn't harm most tarantula species.

- Another tip is that cooler temperatures may lead to slower metabolism and slower growth though this is not entirely bad for a sling.

Stages of Molting

Stage 1: Intermolt

This is the stage where the bird eating spider or tarantulas in general are still eating normally anytime your feed and behaving normally as this is part of the growing process. This is where your pet is doing their usual routines and still quite active. You'll also notice that the abdomen skin of the spider is pale which is in its normal shade.

Stage 2: Proecdysis

This is the next stage of the molting process. This is when the molt is imminent. The spider's body will start pumping fluids in the 2 sets of its exoskeletons to get the body ready to molt. This is the point where your bird eating spider is ready to fully undergo through the molting process.

Stage 3: Ecdysis

This is the molting proper. It is the part where the tarantula will expand itself to pop its limbs and work its way out of the molt. This process can take many hours to at least 1 day depending on the current size of your bird eating spider.

Stage 4: Postecdysis

This is the stage where the bird eating spider is already folding its new exoskeleton. You'll see the skin filling out and hardening, you'll also see it stretching. The fangs at this point is delicately soft that's why it won't be able to eat. You should wait for at least a few days to a couple of weeks before you offer them food.

Signs of Molting

- Sign #1: Your pet stops eating
- Sign #2: Your pet will develop a large and dark or shiny abdomen
- Sign #3: Your pet will become more lethargic
- Sign #4: Your pet will bury itself underground
- Sign #5: Your pet will lay down a molting mat

Index

E

F

G

H

I

L

Photo Credits

Page 1 Photo by user Allan Hopkins via Flickr.com,

https://www.flickr.com/photos/hoppy1951/10174035894/

Page 4 Photo by user Brian Gratwicke via Flickr.com,

https://www.flickr.com/photos/briangratwicke/30775431403/

Page 14 Photo by user Ryan Somma via Flickr.com,

https://www.flickr.com/photos/ideonexus/2419335033/

Page 24 Photo by user Leah via Flickr.com,

https://www.flickr.com/photos/lcheady/3416425481/

Page 31 Photo by user Mickey Champion via Flickr.com,

https://www.flickr.com/photos/dogsnewclothes/473004103/

Page 41 Photo by user Patricia Litton via Flickr.com,

https://www.flickr.com/photos/plitton/8001880058/

Page 49 Photo by user Peter via Flickr.com,

https://www.flickr.com/photos/peteredin/2967035811/

Page 56 Photo by user Smithsonian's National Zoo via Flickr.com,

https://www.flickr.com/photos/nationalzoo/7652114612/

Page 64 Photo by user Jon Rawlinson via Flickr.com,

https://www.flickr.com/photos/london/3592381867/

Page 74 Photo by user Brian Gratwicke via Flickr.com,

https://www.flickr.com/photos/briangratwicke/31585241005/

Page 80 Photo by user Allan Hopkins via Flickr.com,

https://www.flickr.com/photos/hoppy1951/8271634237/

References

Goliath Bird Eater - Wikipedia.org

https://en.wikipedia.org/wiki/Goliath_birdeater

Goliath Bird-eating Spider: Goliath Tarantuala, Goliath Birdeater – Animal - World.com

http://animal-world.com/encyclo/reptiles/spiders/GoliathBirdEatingSpider.php

Goliath bird-eating spider - SpidersWorlds.com

http://www.spidersworlds.com/goliath-bird-eater-spider/

Goliath bird-eating spider: The Eight Legged Giant of the Amazon - AboutAnimals.com

https://www.aboutanimals.com/arachnid/goliath-bird-eating-spider/

Goliath bird-eating spider (Theraphosa blondi) - Arkive.org

https://www.arkive.org/goliath-bird-eating-spider/theraphosa-blondi/

Goliath Bird-eating Spider – Blue Planet Biomes

http://www.blueplanetbiomes.org/goliath_bird_eating_spider.htm

Molting - TarantulaGuide.com

https://www.tarantulaguide.com/tarantula-molting/

Tarantula - Kellyvillepets.com.au

https://www.kellyvillepets.com.au/pages/bird-eating-spiders

Tarantula Molting - TarantulaPets.com

http://www.tarantulapets.com/tarantula-molting/

Tarantula Sling Husbandry – A Comprehensive Guide - TomsBigSpiders.com

https://tomsbigspiders.com/2016/08/26/tarantula-sling-husbandry/

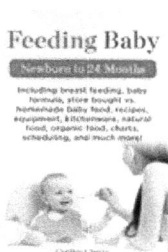

Feeding Baby
Cynthia Cherry
978-1941070000

Axolotl
Lolly Brown
978-0989658430

Dysautonomia, POTS
Syndrome
Frederick Earlstein
978-0989658485

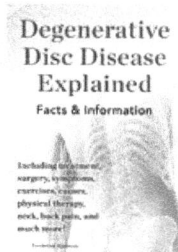

Degenerative Disc
Disease Explained
Frederick Earlstein
978-0989658485

Sinusitis, Hay Fever,
Allergic Rhinitis Explained
Frederick Earlstein
978-1941070024

Wicca
Riley Star
978-1941070130

Zombie Apocalypse
Rex Cutty
978-1941070154

Capybara
Lolly Brown
978-1941070062

Eels As Pets
Lolly Brown
978-1941070167

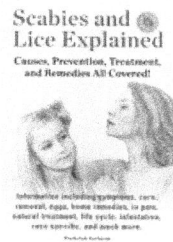

Scabies and Lice Explained
Frederick Earlstein
978-1941070017

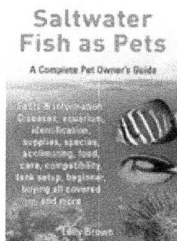

Saltwater Fish As Pets
Lolly Brown
978-0989658461

Torticollis Explained
Frederick Earlstein
978-1941070055

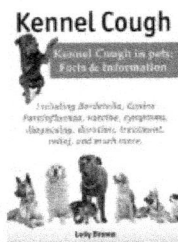

Kennel Cough
Lolly Brown
978-0989658409

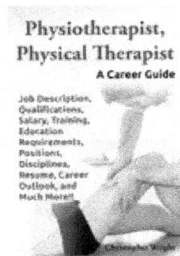

Physiotherapist, Physical
Therapist
Christopher Wright
978-0989658492

Rats, Mice, and Dormice
As Pets
Lolly Brown
978-1941070079

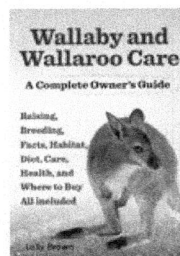

Wallaby and Wallaroo Care
Lolly Brown
978-1941070031

Bodybuilding Supplements
Explained
Jon Shelton
978-1941070239

Demonology
Riley Star
978-19401070314

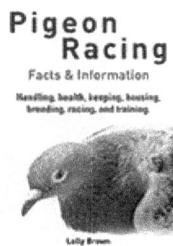

Pigeon Racing
Lolly Brown
978-1941070307

Dwarf Hamster
Lolly Brown
978-1941070390

Cryptozoology
Rex Cutty
978-1941070406

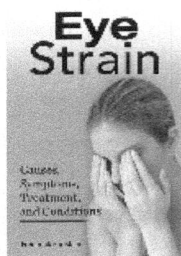

Eye Strain
Frederick Earlstein
978-1941070369

Inez The Miniature Elephant
Asher Ray
978-1941070353

Vampire Apocalypse
Rex Cutty
978-1941070321

www.ingramcontent.com/pod-product-compliance
Lightning Source LLC
Chambersburg PA
CBHW072007060426

42446CB00042B/2016